A Framework for Young Children's Spiritual Capabilities

DR CHRISTINE ROBINSON,
DR BRENDAN HYDE & DR MEGAN BEST

Copyright © 2024 by Dr Christine Robinson, Dr Brendan Hyde & Dr Megan Best
All rights reserved.

No portion of this book may be reproduced in any form without written permission from the publisher or author, except as permitted by copyright law.

This publication is designed to provide accurate and authoritative information in regard to the subject matter covered. It is sold with the understanding that neither the author nor the publisher is engaged in rendering legal, investment, accounting or other professional services. While the publisher and author have used their best efforts in preparing this book, they make no representations or warranties with respect to the accuracy or completeness of the contents of this book and specifically disclaim any implied warranties of merchantability or fitness for a particular purpose.

No warranty may be created or extended by sales representatives or written sales materials. The advice and strategies contained herein may not be suitable for your situation. You should consult with a professional when appropriate. Neither the publisher nor the author shall be liable for any loss of profit or any other commercial damages, including but not limited to special, incidental, consequential, personal, or other damages.

Authors

Dr Christine Robinson
Christine is Associate Professor in Early Childhood at the University of Notre Dame Australia. Christine has taught within early childhood before entering academia where she now teaches and researches various topics within the early years. In particular Christine's work focuses on the role of spirituality in young children's development and education; play and play-based pedagogies; teacher formation and curriculum.

Dr Brendan Hyde
Brendan is a Senior Lecturer in the School of Education at Deakin University, and Chair of the International Association for Children's Spirituality. He has researched in children's spirituality for more than 20 years and has an international reputation in this field. Brendan also holds an honorary position at the Centre for the Theology of Childhood, presently located in Denver, Colorado.

Dr Megan Best
Associate Professor Megan Best is a Research Associate with the Institute for Ethics and Society at the University of Notre Dame Australia. She has a clinical background in Palliative Medicine. A/Professor Best's research interests include spirituality in healthcare, existential suffering, psycho-oncology, whole person care and bioethics. A/Professor Best has published extensively in her field.

Acknowledgements

The authors wish to acknowledge the contribution of MercyCare in enabling the development of this Framework. Thank you to the MercyCare leadership team and to the centre educators for sharing in our passion for young children's spirituality.

Research

This Framework has been developed as a result of the research of the three authors over a period of 20 years. The Framework has been informed by this research and contributes new research to the field by positioning itself as a guide for practice in early childhood education and care.

What is Spirituality?

Why a Framework for Young Children's Spiritual Capabilities?

This Framework aims to provide a resource for educators working with children in early childhood contexts in Australia. The early years are recognised as being from birth to age eight, and these years are critical for laying the foundations for thriving into adulthood (Australian Government, 2024). To thrive, children need a focus on their whole self. Children need to feel safe, secure, connected and to be enabled to play, imagine and grow holistically (Australian Government, 2024).

This Framework draws on research that is clear in advocating for children's spirituality to be nurtured and promoted as part of a 'whole child approach' (National Scientific Council on the Developing Child. (2004). There are many positive outcomes when children have their spiritual capacity invested in. Spirituality contributes to positive functioning in childhood and promotes positive health behaviours (Bryant-Davis et al, 2012; Rew et al., 2004). By nurturing spirituality, educators can increase children's self-confidence and self-esteem (Adams et al., 2008). Spirituality underlies the relationships which provide the child with a sense of belonging, inspiring in them a sense of purpose and providing a framework of meaning within which they come to understand their everyday experiences, find their place in the world and seek answers to the big questions in life (de Souza 2016).

By explicitly distilling the existing research on what spirituality is, this Framework contributes new and innovative ways of perceiving spirituality from a capabilities perspective. Opportunities for spiritual affordances in early childhood contexts are suggested for each capability. It's important to note that the capabilities are not a set of requirements, but rather affordances educators can offer to children. Our hope is that educators find this a useful resource for promoting and nurturing young children's innate spirituality.

Section One

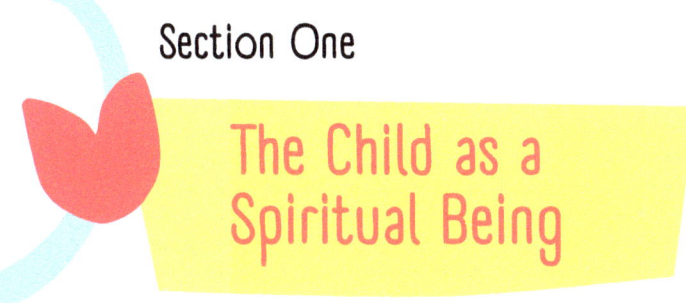

The Child as a Spiritual Being

A holistic perspective of the child

A holistic perspective of the child emphasises the inter-connectedness of the developmental domains, acknowledging that attending to the cognitive, physical, social-emotional *and* spiritual domains of development are *all* essential to human thriving (Robinson, 2024). A holistic perspective attends to the child in their fullness and recognises that development and learning don't occur in adult constructed learning areas, but rather through experiences which engage the whole self.

Spirituality as distinct from religion

Spirituality is not the same as religion. While historically spirituality has been tied to religion, contemporary research has come to understand the distinctive nature of spirituality. Spirituality and religion are described as dichotomous constructs that intersect for individuals who identify as religious. So for some people, spirituality is expressed through religious beliefs, and for others, it is not.

Spirituality is innate. The spiritual capacity is also part of what makes a person human and integral to a holistic view of personhood.

A 'working definition' of spirituality

Spirituality is innate to the human person. It is capacity for self-transcendence in which a person participates in the sacred – something greater than the self. It propels the search for connectedness, meaning, purpose, and ethical responsibility. It is experienced, formed, shaped and expressed through a wide range of narratives, beliefs and practices, and is shaped by many influences in family, community, society, culture and nature.

Section One

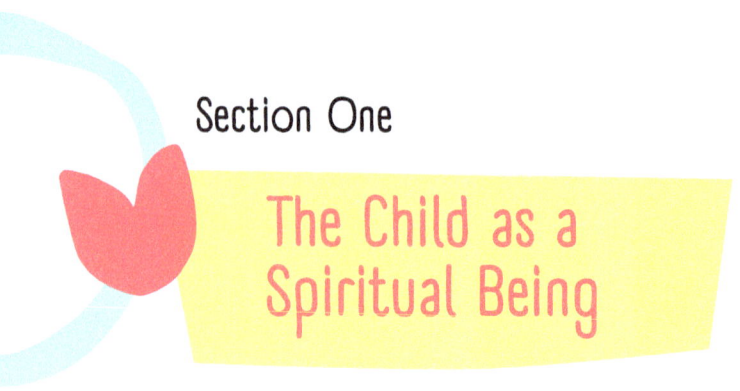

The Child as a Spiritual Being

Mandates Contextualising the Australian Early Years Context

The Early Years Learning Framework [EYLF] (AGDE, 2022) is the guiding mandated document for pedagogy in Australian early years' contexts. The EYLF promotes spirituality as one part of the whole child. Spirituality is a capacity that requires attending to, alongside the other development domains. Specifically, the EYLF (AGDE, 2022) states spirituality as referring "to a range of human experiences including a sense of awe and wonder, or peacefulness, and an exploration of being and knowing" (p. 68) and this understanding of spirituality is built upon in this Framework.

In addition to the EYLF, for those children in school settings, the Australian Curriculum (Australian Curriculum and Assessment Reporting Authority [ACARA], 2024), informed by the Alice Springs Declaration (Education Council, 2019), mandates curriculum that includes a focus on general capabilities. The Australian Curriculum (ACARA) articulates seven capabilities that overarch the curriculum areas and seek to promote the development of the whole person in relation to the world around them.

The development of this Framework for Young Children's Spiritual Capabilities resides within this specific context and aims to complement the holistic, relational and play-based focus of the EYLF (AGDE, 2022) whilst aligning to the vision of the Australian Curriculum to develop competent, capable and thriving citizens.

HOW THE FRAMEWORK IS STRUCTURED

FRAMING THE CAPABILITY

The way in which spirituality is experienced and expressed in the early years has been used to frame a capability. There are eight capabilities in the Framework that aim to focus the educator on what children are able to do.

INFORMED BY RESEARCH

The capabilities have been developed as a result of comprehensive research on the ways children might experience and express their spirituality. The research drawn upon for each capability is provided as background for the educator.

CAPABILITY IN ACTION

Practical suggestions are provided in relation to each capability. Sometimes these suggestions are for intentionally planning opportunities for spirituality. Sometimes the suggestions are for building on and responding to child initiated moments.

Section Two

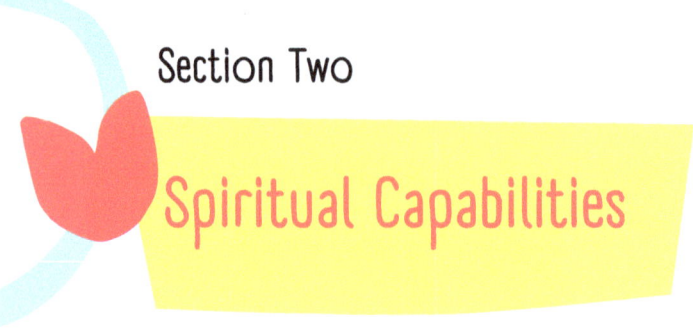

Spiritual Capabilities

A Focus on Capabilities

This Framework has adopted a focus on capabilities as a way to frame how educators can promote and nurture children's innate spirituality. In constructing capabilities, spirituality can be expressed in terms of the "knowledge, skills, behaviours and dispositions" (ACARA, 2013, p. 5.) we hope for children to develop. When children successfully develop these capabilities it means they can live out and apply this knowledge, skill, behaviour or disposition confidently, effectively and appropriately in complex and changing circumstances (ACARA, 2013, p. 5).

Structuring the Framework in relation to capabilities aligns to the vision of the child as one who is capable, possessing agency and voice as they navigate their own learning and development. Capabilities are about what children can do, how they behave and the dispositions they grow. Spirituality belongs to the child, and when viewed from a capability perspective, attends to the holistic nature of education.

A capabilities focus for promoting young children's spirituality recognises "the child is a multidimensional being...encased in the physical body which allows the individual child to engage, mediate and interact with the world around them" (de Souza, 2016, p. 123).

The Role of the Educator in Promoting Children's Spirituality

Research suggests that educators promote and nurture spirituality in the ways that they themselves experience it (Robinson, 2020). For example, the educator who experiences spirituality through nature, tends to promote nature experiences for their children. Whilst this is a good first step, educators require knowledge about all the ways spirituality can be experienced and expressed in order to meet the needs of all children. The role of the educator is explicitly addressed for each capability presented in the Framework to assist a more intentional approach to affording children spiritual opportunities.

Section Two

Capability Statement: I can wonder and imagine possibilities

Informed by Research
Wondering is described as the ability to enter into amazement; to contemplate the perplexity and mystery of the world and all within it (Piersol, 2014). Children are naturally curious and engage innately with wonder (Fuller, 2006). When children wonder, they do so holistically, drawing on all of their capacities and senses to explore possibilities and to be consumed in a moment of time that facilitates feelings of joy, peace and happiness (Mata-McMahon, Haslip & Shein, 2019). When wonder, as a characteristic of spirituality, isn't valued and nurtured, it can be lost into adulthood (Carson, 1965; Robinson, 2019).

Wonder in action: 0-3 years
- Include sensory play: varying materials and textures, mirrors, natural objects
- Provide outdoor play opportunities in nature
- Include natural materials in indoor play spaces
- Model the posing of 'wonder questions' in relation to the natural environment. Eg *Wow, look at that wonderful rainbow?*

Wonder in action: 4-8 years
- Construct a Wonder Wall or a Wonder Table: add children's wonderings to the wall for others to explore, or add objects to the table.
- Model wondering and pose wonder questions for children to consider
- Provide nature-based play opportunities that afford time and space

The Role of the Educator
Children are natural wonderers - they lead the way for us! Wonder doesn't require an answer, but a companion. As educators, we are called to enter into the wonder of the child. Share in the moment by being present to the child or by posing a wondering of your own. Sometimes, promoting wonder as a part of children's spirituality means leaving them to it, rather than interrupting or moving them onto a more obvious learning task. The educators role in wonder is to value it and acknowledge it.

Section Two

I am part of the world

Capability Statement: I can connect with the world

Informed by Research
Children possess an innate interest and affiliation with the natural world, and when promoted, this can become a life-long ability to both connect, as a component of spirituality, and to contribute back to the world through appreciation and care for it. A care for the world comes from a connection to it. Research explains that a characteristic of spirituality is experiencing and expressing a sense of connectedness with the natural world (Harris, 2016; Louv, 2012). Feeling connected to nature contributes positively to children's feelings of happiness and overall well-being. Experiencing a sense of connection with nature can promote identity development and feelings of belonging (Lee-Hammond, 2017; Robinson, 2019). Nature has a way of offering stability when life is uncertain, and is often a source of meaning and purpose in life (Howell et al., 2013, p. 1683).

Nature in action: 0-3 years
- Include natural materials for indoor play
- Spend time outdoors engaged in nature play experiences
- Share your own love and appreciation for nature
- Pose wonder questions in connection to wonder
- Afford children time and space in nature

Nature in action: 4-8 years
- Spend time outdoors engaged in nature play outdoors
- Share your own love and appreciation for nature
- Encourage care for the natural world through respect
- Encourage care for the natural world through sustainable practices
- Pose wonder questions in connection to wonder
- Afford children time and space in nature

The Role of the Educator
Promoting children's spirituality through a connection to nature requires an educator who values and respects the world. Modelling an appreciation and respect for nature, along with the intentional affordance of nature-based play opportunities, are central to instilling in children a life-long affiliation with the world. Educators also take the role of facilitator in providing the time and space for nature engagement.

Section Two

I imagine and create

Capability Statement: I can imagine and be creative

Informed by Research
To imagine is to dream, to explore possibilities, to think innovatively and draws on another characteristic of spirituality, wonder. While using one's imagination is largely a cognitive process, the creativity that can follow engages a child holistically as they bring to life their imaginings. Creativity provides children with an avenue to express themselves differently, drawing on how they feel, think and act. Opportunities to imagine and to be creative in the early years, provides a foundation for later life where skills of deep thinking, flexible thinking, innovation and critical thinking are valued; creativity is described as a developmental asset (Pandya, 2024). Spiritually, this capability assists children in expressing not only who they are and how they feel, but who they want to become.

Imagination & Creativity in action: 0-3 years
- Provide choice: vary the materials, play spaces, and mediums for creativity (paint, play-doh, construction materials)
- Provoke children's imagination by offering visual provocations alongside wonder questions (Eg a birds nest, a unicycle)
- Avoid activities that limit children's individual creativity (Eg pre-packaged or worksheet style tasks)

Imagination & Creativity in action: 4-8 years
- Provide choice: vary the materials, play spaces, and mediums for creativity (paint, play-doh, construction materials)
- Provoke children's thinking by offering open-ended questions (Eg posing a problem to be solved) or providing a visual provocation (Eg a birds nest, a unicycle)
- Afford children time to imagine and both space and time to create

The Role of the Educator
Children enjoy imagining and creating. To facilitate this as a spiritual capability means valuing children's agency by providing opportunities for their individual self expression. Recognising the importance of imagination and creativity to children's spirituality, and to their holistic development, will assist the educator in promoting these opportunities. Questioning, facilitating and encouraging children's creativity is a key role for the educator.

Section Two

I can play

Capability Statement: I can play, investigate and solve problems

Informed by Research

In play, children are able to make sense of their world by enacting aspects of their experience without consequence (Robinson, 2024). Play affords children an alternate reality, one where they can re-imagine who they are, how they behave and who they want to become. In this way, play can positively contribute to children's construction of their identity (AGDE, 2022). As a holistic experience, play connects the spiritual capacity with the cognitive, emotional and physical capacities, as children explore, investigate and problem solve in their play scenarios. The sense of connectedness experienced through play can be 'within' and 'without' as children connect not only with who they are, but they explore who they are in relation to others and the world.

Play in action: 0-3 years

- Provide indoor and outdoor play spaces
- Afford children less structured play opportunites that facilitate them self selecting the activity and resources
- Change the play contexts regularly to encourage different types of play

Play & Inquiry in action: 4-8 years

- Provide indoor and outdoor play spaces
- Afford children time to engage in sustained play that develops scenarios and story-lines as this promotes negotiat
- Change the play contexts regularly to encourage different types of play

The Role of the Educator

The role of the educator in children's play is multi-dimensional. The educator is the facilitator and director in that they take a lead role in establishing the context and materials for the play to occur - as well as the time. When the play begins, from an educational perspective there may be many roles, both active and passive, the educator can take. With a focus on spirituality, a more passive presence by the educator is required. This passive presence provides the space children need to explore the scenarios, engage in sustained feeling and thinking and to negotiate and solve the problems that are of significance to them, in that moment.

Section Two

I know who I am now

Capability Statement: I have agency and autonomy

Informed by Research
The development of a strong sense of identity is acknowledged in the EYLF (AGDE, 2022) as a key outcome for children in the early years. Identity development relies on feeling safe and secure. When children feel this way, they learn that who they are is respected and celebrated. In turn, children develop a sense of agency (to make choices) and autonomy (to control actions). A child's identity is formed as they draw on their cultural and/or religious backgrounds, engage in family and community rituals and begin to feel that they belong. In connection to spirituality, the way in which children feel connected to their inner-self, to others, and to the world is tied to the construct of identity as children come to know who they are.

Identity in action: 0-3 years
- Engage families in constructing the child's routines
- Intentionally include the rituals and traditions of the cultures children represent
- Seek to understand the individual child and to respond sensitively to children's uniqueness, encouraging their contributions in all its forms

Identity in action: 4-8 years
- Provide time and space for independent play and learning
- Encourage children to persevere when challenged
- Seek knowledge from families and communities about cultural practices and rituals that can be integrated in your room

The Role of the Educator
The early years provides a natural context for identity development as children come to services and schools with the knowledge and practices of their families. The role of the educator is to seek information, create continuity, and establish a safe and secure environment for the child; an environment that speaks to the child to say 'we see you' and 'you belong here'. When educators provide opportunities for connectedness, opportunities for children to be inward thinking and feeling, as well as developing their sense of belonging, they are promoting children's spirituality.

Section Two

Who will I become?

Capability Statement: I can make meaning from things that happen and find my purpose in life

Informed by Research

Childhood is a time to seek and make meaning of the world (AGDE, 2022). Making meaning and searching for purpose in life accord with the 'working definition' of spirituality presented in this Framework. Children's meaning making is continuous and can be a way they express their spirituality. It enables them to make meaningful connections with self, others, the world, and God (Hyde, 2008). Research suggests that having a sense of meaning and purpose in life promotes feelings of happiness and helps children to thrive.

Meaning & Purpose in action: 0-3 years

- Become familiar with the sources from which children make meaning and discuss these with them (eg family and cultural identity)
- Provide opportunities for children to talk and draw about what matters to them.
- Create safe spaces for children in which they can express their meaning and purpose

Meaning & Purpose in action: 4-8 years

- Use strategies such as 'circle time' to create safe spaces in which children can express their meaning making
- Encourage children to make meaning from stories, songs, television, and discuss this intentionally with them
- Afford children time to reflect on meaning and what it might mean for them

The Role of the Educator

Becoming familiar with how children make meaning, and taking these seriously, is a challenge. Providing safe spaces to do this is important. Documents such as the EYLF (AGDE, 2022) can assist educators to intentionally include opportunities for meaning making in their planning. Children make meaning in many different ways. It is important that adults are sensitive and respectful of the child's meaning making, and where appropriate, partner with children in this process.

Section Two

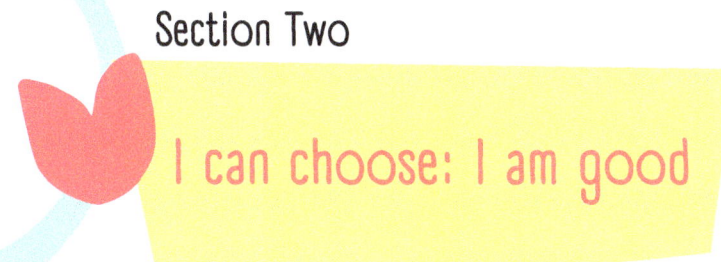

I can choose: I am good

Capability Statement: I make good choices, act fairly and know what is right

Informed by Research

Morals and the construction of personal values are tied to spirituality. Children are built to know good and bad; right and wrong (Miller, 2015). Coming to a sense of identity, and understanding one's meaning and purpose in life are enhanced as a child develops values and morals by which to live (Ng & Lu, 2015). In early childhood, the development of morals and values are facilitated by being in an educational community whereby guidelines for fairness, justice, behaviour and attitudes are modelled, taught and formed. Children grow their sense of self in relation to others, and in doing so, learn how to live and act alongside others in ways that promote good choices, acts of kindness, a sense of fairness and what is 'right'.

Values and morals in action: 0-3 years

- Read children's literature to teach the concept of 'good choices'
- Create the room/class behaviour guidelines around choices, ecouraging 'good choices'

Values and morals in action: 4-8 years

- Read children's literature that presents ethical or moral dilemmas to open up discussion on topics of right and wrong.
- Create the room/class guidelines and expectations together as a group to enable children to consider how their actions impact others
- When children make a poor choice, provide time for them to reflect on how their choice feels for them, and for others. Reflection on action is a useful skill for children to learn.

The Role of the Educator

The educator takes a leading role in assisting children with this capability. Whilst children have a natural interest in ethical dilemmas of fairness and justice, the educator must model and explicitly teach values and morals to young children. Taking the spontaneous opportunities that arise is an appropriate way to engage children in moments of teaching about values. Children will look to how the educator applies their own values, and is consistent with them, to know if they are authentic.

Section Two

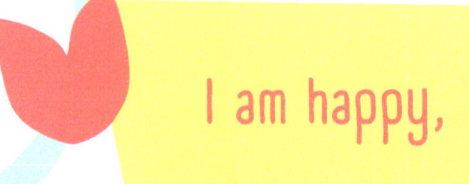

I am happy, I laugh

Capability Statement: I experience joy and humour

Informed by Research
Feelings of happiness are associated with joy and humour. The experience of joy and humour can be brought about for many reasons. Mata-McMahon's (2017) research with young children found that joy and humour came about from experiencing music, kindness and compassion, using one's imagination and through caring relationships. From a spiritual perspective, all of these experiences that lead to joy, humour and happiness provide a connection to the self and to others. When children feel happy, they learn and develop. When children feel happy, they can be in the here and now (Nye, 2014) and they can imagine a future with meaning and purpose. "Happy people are better able to deal with the adversities that are a part of life" (Schein, 2018, p. 80)

Joy and humour in action: 0-3 years
- Share humorous stories / literature with children
- Engage in imaginative tasks with children and add in 'lighter' elements to draw out children's sense of joy and laughter
- Build on what children find amusing - use their initiatives to be funny to share in moments of joy with them.

Joy and humour in action: 4-8 years
- Share humorous literature with children and talk to them about what they find funny
- Provide opportunities to share moments of happiness - what brings them joy? What makes them happy? Encourage conversations about how they can draw on this when times are tough
- Model the use of joy and humour as a way to connect to others to build relationships, and to self by way of creating a positive outlook on life.

The Role of the Educator
The educator takes a leading role in modelling to children how to experience joy and humour in life. Laughing with children, sharing in funny moments and using humour as a way to help overcome 'tough times' can illustrate to children a way to engage their spiritual self through connection to self and others.

Section Two

I am still; I reflect

Capability Statement: I can be thoughtful and reflective

Informed by Research

Children lead busy lives. Affording opportunities for quiet, for rest, for thoughtfulness and reflection can all positively promote children's spirituality. It is in the quiet and the reflection that children can become attuned to their 'inner voice', their deepest feelings and thoughts. Nye (2014) affirms the importance of silence in children's life - silence doesn't mean nothing is happening, rather silence provides an openness to listening to the head and the heart. When children learn how to be in silence, and to engage reflectively, they further develop their connection to their 'self'.

Silence and reflection in action: 0-3 years

- Provide time for quiet in the day, this could include playing reflective music
- Create a quiet space in the room that is furnished with a place to rest, look at a book or listen to reflective music independently

Silence and reflection in action: 4-8 years

- Lead children through a guided meditation, encouraging them to slow down, and to listen to their inner voice
- Model being inwardly 'thoughtful' eg *Talk out loud your own reflection on how you feel about a situation such as feeling worried, or feeling calm*
- Create a quiet space in the room that is furnished as a place to rest, look at a book or listen to reflective music independently

The Role of the Educator

Taking time out to rest and be reflective doesn't always come easily for children. Educators can offer children these opportunities for thoughtfulness and reflection in a number of ways. Sometimes it can be through the affordance of space inside or outside that provides a place to be alone and quiet. Other times the educator can lead the whole group of children through a guided mediation or through rest time with wonder questions. Modelling how to be reflective, by the educator, is also key.

Section Two

I think there's something more

Capability Statement: I can talk about there being something greater

Informed by Research
In their research, Hay with Nye (2006) identify that children are capable of talking about a Transcendent, or their concept of the Divine, and the meaning and emotion that these prompts. This reflects the findings from Cavalletti (1992) and Berryman (2009) that the Creator is present to young children, who, over time, are able to speak about their relationship with the Creator and how this makes them feel. In relation to spirituality, a sense of connectedness to the Transcendent, or a Creator, is one of the hallmarks of spirituality (Adams et al., 2008; Fisher, 2015; Hay with Nye, 2006; Hyde, 2008; Yust et. al, 2005). For some, this is we where spirituality and religion intersect.

Transcendence in action: 0-3 years
- Enjoy moments of stillness and quiet together
- Share picture story books that include ideas of the Divine
- Sing songs about the Creator, e.g. "I will trust you God" from Kids Worship
- Allow children opportunities to share their 'wonderings'

Transcendence in action: 4-8 years
- Plan times of stillness and solitude, inside and also in nature
- As appropriate, plan opportunities for prayer and worship
- Encourage wonder questions that build on the notion of transcendence eg *I wonder who made the world*
- Begin to introduce an explore language about the Divine.

The Role of the Educator
The educator takes a leading role in modelling to children how to enage in moments of stillness and quiet as a means of connecting to something greater than themselves. As well, the educator plays a critical role in the selection of story books, songs, etc, and also in preparing a safe environment for talking and singing about the Creator - and allowing God to be present to the children in the room. The educator can respond to the religious backgrounds of children by affording them opportunities to provide religion responses that are received positively.

Section Three

Spirituality as a Protective Factor

Spirituality and the 'shadow'

The spiritual capacity is also characterised by the opposite of the capabilities explored in this Framework, for example, disconnectedness, fear, anxiety, depression, sadness. The idea of the 'shadow' is to acknowledge the 'whole person' and all their experiences - the light and the dark (de Souza, 2016). Enabling children to recognise these more negative experiences, and to overcome them, is key to children's thriving and speaks to how spirituality can be viewed as a protective factor in life.

While uncomfortable experiences of connectedness can occur which reflect the darker side of spirituality, the educator can reduce their impact by promoting positive experiences of connectedness which enhance the child's sense of wellbeing (de Souza, 2016). Zehnder and colleagues (2006) found that spirituality contributes to healthier coping in children when dealing with life's challenges.

Spirituality and Well-being

When children experience adversity, including trauma, they are less likely to develop a positive sense of self, a healthy well-being and they often experience disconnection with others (Arigatou International, 2022). When children have developed their spiritual capacity, they are better able to manage such feelings and to seek strategies to overcome them. Spiritual practices and beliefs are associated with better long term outcomes for children, especially for those who have experienced trauma and adversity (Prior & Petra, 2019) and so spirituality is referred to as a protective factor in life. Spirituality is tied to well-being, and is a necessary component of thriving.

Understanding Spirituality as Part of the Whole Child

Spirituality has been clearly identified as an innate element in the human person, implicit in the relational dimension of life. Therefore, in order to prepare children for the world in which they are growing, it is important to address the spiritual dimension as part of the whole child (de Souza, 2016). In the early years of education and care, research informs us of the benefits of attending to children holistically, and to do this, educators must also understand and promote children's spirituality.

Section Four

Resources

Including spiritual learning in early childhood education and care by Nicole Megan Lees Early Childhood Australia Research in Practice Series (available through ECA)

A Toolkit for Children's Spiritual Development
https://childspiritualdevelopment.org/about-the-toolkit/

How can we nurture children's spirituality?
Youtube video:
https://www.youtube.com/watch?v=wTU0lYF896Y

The Early Years Learning Framework
https://www.acecqa.gov.au/sites/default/files/2023-01/EYLF-2022-V2.0.pdf

More Research

Children's Spirituality: What it is and why it matters
By Rebecca Nye

Children's Spirituality in Early Childhood Education: Theory to practice
By Jennifer Mata-McMahon and Patricia Escarfuller

Connections over Compliance
by Lori L. Desautels

The Spiritual Child: The new science on parenting for health and lifelong thriving
by Lisa Miller

Young Children as Spiritual Beings in a Globalised World
Edited by Elizabeth Rouse, Brendan Hyde and Tony Eaude

References

Adams, K., Hyde, B., & Woolley, R. (2008). *The spiritual dimension of childhood*. Jessica Kingsley Publications.

Arigatou International (2022). *Consortium on nurturing values and spirituality in early childhood for the prevention of violence*. https://childspiritualdevelopment.org/2022/11/17/toolkit/

Australian Government. (2024). *Early years strategy 2024-2034*.

Australian Government Department of Education for the Ministerial Council [AGDE]. (2022). *Belonging, being and becoming: The early years learning framework for Australia, (V2.0)*. Australian Government Department of Education for the Ministerial Council.

Australian Curriculum and Assessment Reporting Authority (ACARA), (2013; 2024). *Australian curriculum*.

Berryman, J. (2009). *Teaching Godly Play: How to mentor the spiritual development of children*. Morehouse Education Resources.

Bryant-Davis, T., Ellis, M. U., Burke-Maynard, E., Moon, N., Counts, P. A., & Anderson, G. (2012). Religiosity, spirituality, and trauma recovery in the lives of children and adolescents. *Professional Psychology: Research and Practice, 43*(4), 306.

Carson, R. (1965). *The sense of wonder*. HarperCollins.

Cavalletti, S. (1992). *The religious potential of the child*. Catechesis of the Good Shepherd Publications.

De Souza, M. (2016). *Spirituality in education in a global, pluralised world*. Routledge.

de Souza, M. (2016). The spiritual dimension of education–addressing issues of identity and belonging. *Discourse and Communication for Sustainable Education, 7*(1), 125-138.

Education Council. (2019). *Alice Springs (Mparntwe) education declaration*. Education Council Secretariat.

Fisher, J. (2015). God counts for children's spiritual wellbeing. *International Journal of Children's Spirituality, 20* (3-4), 191-203.

Fuller, R. C. (2006). *Wonder*. University of North Carolina Press.

Hay, D., with Nye, R. (2006). *The spirit of the child* (revised edition). Jessica Kingsley Publishers.

References (Cont...)

Harris K. (2016). Let's play at the park! Family pathways promoting spiritual resources to inspire nature, pretend play, storytelling, intergenerational play and celebrations. International Journal of Children's Spirituality, 21, 90–103.

Howell A. J., Passmore H. A., Buro K. (2013). Meaning in nature: Meaning in life as a mediator of the relationship between nature connectedness and well-being. Journal of Happiness Studies, 14, 1681–1696.

Hyde, B. (2008). *Children and spirituality: Searching for meaning and connectedness.* Jessica Kingsley Publishers.

Louv R. (2012). *The nature principle: Reconnecting with life in a virtual age.* Algonquin Books.

Lee-Hammond L. (2017). Belonging in nature: Spirituality, Indigenous cultures and biophilia. In Waller T., Ärlemalm-Hagsér E., Beate Hansen Sandseter E., Lee-Hammond L., Lekies K. S., Wyver S. (Eds.), *The SAGE handbook of outdoor play and learning.* SAGE.

Mata-McMahon, J. (2017). Spirituality and humour: making connections for early childhood education. *International Journal of Children's Spirituality, 22(2)*, 170–178. https://doi.org/10.1080/1364436X.2017.1287681.

Mata-McMahon, J., M. J. Haslip, and D. L. Schein. (2019). Early Childhood Educators' Perceptions of Nurturing Spirituality in Secular Settings. *Early Child Development and Care 189 (14)*: 2233–2251. doi:10.1080/03004430.2018.1445734.

Miller, L. (2015). *The spiritual child: The neuroscience on parenting for health and lifelong thriving.* St Martin's Press,

Nye, R. (2014). *Children's Spirituality: What it is and why it matters.* Church House Publishing.

National Scientific Council on the Developing Child. (2004). *Children's emotional development is built into the architecture of their brains: Working paper No. 2.* Center on the Developing Child. Harvard University.

Ng, P. T. M., & Lu, L. (2015). Spirituality and morality: a study of communal aspects from eastern and western perspectives. *Journal of Religious Education, 63*(1), 13–24. https://doi.org/10.1007/s40839-015-0016-7.

Pandya, S. P. (2024). AC-2306327-0000001 Spirituality and creativity in the early childhood context. *International Journal of Children's Spirituality, 29*(1), 18–41. https://doi.org/10.1080/1364436X.2023.2265076

References (Cont...)

Piersol, L. (2014). Our hearts leap up: Awakening wonder within the classroom. In K. Egan, A. Cant, and G. Judson (Eds.), *Wonder-full Education: The Centrality of Wonder in Teaching and Learning across the Curriculum* (pp. 11-29). Routledge.

Prior, M.K. & Petra, M. (2019). Assessing the effects of childhood multitype maltreatment on adult spirituality. *Journal of Child and Adolescent Trauma 13*, 469-480. https://doi.org/10.1007/s40653-019-00288-8

Rew, L., Wong, Y. J., & Sternglanz, R. W. (2004). The relationship between prayer, health behaviors, and protective resources in school-age children. *Issues in Comprehensive Pediatric Nursing, 27*(4), 245-255.

Robinson, C. (2019). Young Children's Spirituality: A Focus on Engaging with Nature. Australasian Journal of Early Childhood 44 (4): 339–350. https://doi.org/10.1177/1836939119870907.

Robinson, C. (2020). To be 'formed' and 'informed': Early years' educators' perspectives of spirituality and its affordance in faith-based early learning centres. *International Journal of Children's Spirituality, 25* (3-4), 254-271.

Schein, D. (2018). *Inspiring wonder, awe and empathy: Spiritual development in young children*. Redleaf Press.

Robinson, C., & Williams, H. (2024). Interpretative phenomenological analysis: Learnings from employing IPA as a qualitative methodology in educational research. *The Qualitative Report, 29*(7), 939-952.

Robinson, C. (2024). Reframing Play through the Spiritual Lens. In E. Rouse, B. Hyde and T. Eaude (Eds), Nurturing Young Children as Spiritual Beings in a Globalised World. Bloomsbury Press. https://www.bloomsbury.com/uk/nurturing-young-children-as-spiritual-beings-in-a-globalized-world-9781350411722/

Yust, K-M., Johnson, A.N., Eisenberg Sasso, S., & Roehlkepartain, E.C. (Eds.). (2005). Nurturing child and adolescent spirituality: Perspectives from the world's religious traditions. Rowman & Littlefield Publishers

Zehnder, D., Prchal, A., Vollrath, M., & Landolt, M. A. (2006). Prospective study of the effectiveness of coping in pediatric patients. *Child psychiatry and human development, 36*, 351-368

www.ingramcontent.com/pod-product-compliance
Lightning Source LLC
Chambersburg PA
CBHW040639100526
44585CB00039B/2874